STORM FORCE

The Westcountry's Wild Winter of 1989/90

1. You could hardly breathe, let alone stand, when the hurricane struck — a schoolgirl struggles to cross the Tamar Bridge.

Derek Lean
Environment Editor of the Western Morning News

– Contents –

2. A driver squeezes through a hazard he could never have expected at Budleigh Salterton.

First published 1990
– Archive Publications Ltd –
10 Seymour Court
Manor Park
RUNCORN
Cheshire

in association with

Western Morning News
Leicester Harmsworth House, 65 New George Street
PLYMOUTH
PL1 1RE

ISBN 0 948946 78 4

– Foreword –

By Sir Ian Amory, chairman of the National Trust Committee for Devon and Cornwall.

This book will be a vivid reminder through its pictures and words of the disastrous occurrences during the winter of 1989/90.

We had the sea flooding of December which did damage to so much of the area and National Trust coastal properties, and then the storms of January 25 followed by further gales in February which were another blow to gardeners and others who had struggled to clear signs of earlier devastation.

It was a whole series of events which meant the National Trust and so many others in the region have suffered grievously in many ways. Now it will take generations to restore the great gardens to the way we remember them from the summer of 1989.

This winter's storms in the South West have been unprecedented in living memory because we luckily escaped the worst of the hurricane of 1987.

But I have toured the Trust's properties of the area and there are plenty of places in the region which reflect the battlefield-like scenes we witnessed in the South East as a result of the great storms there.

After the 1987 storm, the Trust's storm disaster appeal raised £2 million. It is vital that again the public and members of the Trust are as generous as they can be to enable the damage to be cleared up as quickly as possible.

Some of the photographs in this book show magnificent individual specimens which have been lost and underline the enormous amount of work there is to be done. It will take years to get back to normal, but there is the resilience and the will to do so among the people of the peninsula.

Donations to The National Trust Trees and Gardens Storm Disaster Appeal can be sent to:

Freepost
Melksham
Wilts
SN12 6BR

above: Sir Ian Amory

3. **left:** *The huge job of cutting up the fallen trees at lovely Lanhydrock, in Cornwall.*

4. **above:** *Porthleven's battered and broken harbourside wall looked as if a bomb had dropped.*

5. **below:** *Crashing breakers smash at Plymouth's West Hoe under the sullen skies.*

– The Savage Sea –

Nine days before the last Christmas of the decade, seasonal shoppers scurried beneath crowded canopies of festive lights, heading for the sanctuary of home. It was obvious by dusk on that evening of Saturday, December 16, 1989 that the South West was in for a "dirty night". As things turned out, devastating destruction was to be a more accurate description.

Already the wind was exercising its lungs — as it had been for some days — breathing squally gusts of driving rain with a mischievous malevolence into the faces of those package-laden consumers in the towns and cities of Devon and Cornwall.

All afternoon along the south coast, from the Scillies to Seaton Bay and beyond, beneath leaden clouds, low as a frown of fury, the swollen seas roared, tossing and turning into a mounting tumult of anger.

Those who know well the mysterious moods of the sea — it is as if the very sound it makes is different — again cast anxious eyes at the strength of its surge. It had been worryingly rough for some days, and the forecast was of a deep and vigorous depression south west of Ireland moving east to bring storm force winds. Television weather maps were a cobwebbed swirl of tightly packed isobars.

The surge had been noticeable for some time and the height of the tides had increased. According to the tables it should have been a tide of just over 18 feet at Newlyn that morning. It was, in fact, approaching 20 feet 6 inches, which, according to statistics, should happen once in 50 years.

Quickly the power of the wind increased, whipping the sea into a foaming cauldron, a spectacular reminder of Monserrat's famous title, *The Cruel Sea*. Accelerator flat down — or had it really reached the floor? — the wind stormed at Pendennis Castle to register 121 miles per hour.

That, so the statisticians tell us, should occur once in 200 years, but then, in this capricious winter of '89/90 figures, like the weather, were going to be turned topsy-turvy.

On that dark, dreadful night the sea unleashed its full frightening force with a savage intensity the like of which few could recall. Towering waves dashed against cliffs to explode in a

6. The swirling, sullen sea surges against the harbour at wave-battered Porthleven.

5

cascading, crashing foam; they hurled themselves at harbour walls and esplanades; they dashed and dug away at sea defences; they moved granite boulders like marbles and tossed tons of shingle into the air like a blizzard of gritty snow.

Lands End coastguards at Gwennap Head said the spray from the giant waves was soaring above their lookout position 220 feet above sea level. At Mousehole, that lovely little village that gave birth to the legend of "starry gazy pie" and shed its tears on a similar night close to Christmas in 1981 when eight of its men who crewed the Penlee lifeboat, *Solomon Brown*, perished, those waves thundered 50 feet high over the quay.

Harbour master Frank Wallis reported: "The sea came in like mountains and half the car park went." Larger fishing boats parked on the shore were even moved by the might of the remorseless battering, while many of the little craft simply sunk. As for huge baulks of timber across the harbour mouth, they were just snapped in half like matchsticks.

As the South West was pummelled and beaten that fearful night it was West Cornwall that bore the brunt of the assault, but from the Bay of Biscay to the Firth of Clyde there was danger and destruction by the storm which rekindled memories of the "hurricane" of 1987 from which the South West escaped relatively unscathed. Not this time, though.

No more spectacular scenes were depicted than those captured by the camera at Porthleven where next day Mounts Bay was still a maelstrom of menace.

7. Firemen keep an anxious watch on the approaching storm on the Plymouth waterfront.

8. **above:** *The bridge wall of the well-known fishing port of Newlyn was breached, causing flooding and the evacuation of families.*

9. **left:** *The surge of sea caused by the storm brought higher tides than predicted, and floods to Plymouth's Barbican.*

10. **opposite page:** Always a sense of humour, even in adversity. The sign in a sandbagged shop at Cadgwith.

11. **above:** Make do and mend for this keen photographer at West Looe — plastic bags instead of wellies.

12. **left:** A long night for workmen trying to clear roads at Plympton.

How this, the most southerly port in Britain, suffered at the hands of an attacking foaming adversary it knew only too well. The coastline around here has been fairly littered with wrecks over the centuries. Just outside the village on the eastern end of Loe Bar is a simple white cross on grassy slopes, a memorial to HMS *Anson*, a victim of another venomous storm like this. That too happened around Christmas, and the frigate was wrecked with the loss of about 100 lives.

One of the witnesses to the tragedy of 1807 was a Helston man called Henry Trengrouse, who, so the story goes, with the stricken vessel so close, pondered on how people could be rescued in such circumstances. And he it was who invented the rocket and safety line which was in years to come to snatch so many from crippled ships and bring them ashore.

Mercifully this gale claimed no Westcountry lives — alas, a situation tragically to change within a short time of the arrival of 1990 — but dreadful damage was a legacy of monumental proportions. Dozens of merchant ships took refuge in Falmouth, St Ives, and other harbours around the coast seeking shelter on this foul night.

Sunday's dawn revealed the extent of the wounds. Porthleven, said one eye-witness, looked as if it had been struck by a bomb. Roads were closed as broken slates littered the ground and rooftops were draped with a mixture of seaweed and shingle. The massive protective timber baulks placed in position as part of the defences of the inner harbour, and even the granite posts, had been tossed onto the quayside like matchwood.

Still that wind was raging as people discovered just how bad the night had been. Local fishmonger, John Strike, a Porthleven man all his life, said: "It was the worst storm here anybody can remember. Conditions around the harbour were horrendous. In places it looked like the blitz." The analogy was to be repeated many times in the weeks to come.

13. A couple caught out at Seaton esplanade by a massive wave.

In front of the *Ship Inn* the sea wall had been washed away and the slate roof of the old lifeboat house peeled off as easily as a banana skin. Mr Strike, sadly surveying the flattened storage tanks on the quay in which he kept his shellfish, echoed everyone's sentiments as he reflected: "It is truly amazing that no lives were lost. That is the only good thing about this disaster."

Just down the coast at Marazion the destruction of part of the sea wall there meant that suddenly Tony and Pam Manasseh found themselves literally teetering on a precipice. Because of the damage, the breakfast room and part of the dining room of their home was undermined to the extent that parts of the wall were left virtually "floating" in the air.

As workmen toiled to shore up the end of The White House, overlooking St Michael's Mount, Mr Manasseh described a time of tingling tension. "The damage came with Saturday night's high tide. The rain was lashing and the sea was coming over the top of the roof as it had been for two days. We had never known such persistently bad weather. At around 8.30 pm there was a terrific thump and the house shook. I looked out of the window and could see the white of the sea. The carpet was lifted up by the wind coming up through the floorboards.

"I looked over the terrace and the corner of the room was hanging over the sea. It was an enormous wall, 25 feet high and 80 feet long. Now there is just a gaping hole. Everything had gone except for ten feet at the west end," he said.

Every part of this lovely coastline had its story to tell. A small lighthouse on the Duchy of Cornwall-owned quay at St Mary's just disappeared in the storm, and a fireman had the closest call he will ever want when he was lifted bodily into the water, knocked 15 feet out into the sea, but hauled ashore unscathed. The wild and wilful wind showed no respect for property or person. Even the tombstones in the churchyard of St Winwalloe, sitting in the dunes beside the beach, were just ripped out of the ground.

Further up the coast Looe, with its labyrinth of narrow lanes, suffered havoc as it was raked by the combination of rain, tide and wind. Flood water surged through tiny alleyways and dozens of homes and shops in Fore Street were inundated to a depth of two feet. As if the water was not enough, there was sewage too in Fore Street as the volume of the floods pushed up manhole covers and came up through the drains.

14. These boots were made for Christmas shopping at Looe.

Plymouth saw its share of both misery and drama with the historic frigate bearing the city's name, HMS *Plymouth*, being torn by the howling winds from her berth. She was badly holed when she hit the jetty during the height of the gale and a number of her compartments were flooded. This veteran of the Falklands War was saved from the rocks through the skill of a navy tug and one nylon rope. Mike Critchley, director of the Warship Preservation Trust, observed with a succinct lecture in history: "HMS *Plymouth* survived four Argentine bombs in 1982, a major fire in 1986 and, in recent weeks, a plan by the Ministry of Defence to sink her as a missile target. Now the South West storms have done their best to wreck her." Like the rest, they failed.

15. **left:** *Sheer determination — Keith Gaine hard at work when the gangway buckled aboard HMS Plymouth as the storm raged.*

16. **above:** *The fight goes on in the teeth of a gale to secure Falklands veteran, HMS Plymouth.*

17. **above:** *In storm force winds tugs hold a Britanny ferry against the jetty at Plymouth.*

18. **right:** *The skill of a tug's crew and a nylon rope saved HMS Plymouth which was torn from its berth in the city of its name.*

19. **above:** *The road is not the place to park a crabber, but at Cadgwith the storms just pitched it there.*

20. **left:** *Gaping holes in the roof of Plymouth's Waterfront Restaurant where the storms caused thousands of pounds of damage.*

21. **above:** *The dramatic scene at night in Plymouth to make sure of the safety of HMS Plymouth.*
22. **right:** *Water, water everywhere — tidal flooding at Sutton Harbour, Plymouth.*

23. **right:** A tricky crossing for passengers on the Torpoint ferry.

24. **below:** Not only the sea caused problems at coastal resorts. Emergency workers try to dig out a car buried by sand and shingle at Teignmouth.

25. **opposite page:** Sidmouth's Inshore Rescue Services boat house was wrecked by the storms.

Plymouth indeed reverberated to the sound and fury of the storm, and later shared the heartbreak and hard slogging to try and put things right. Business houses on the Barbican suffered badly despite the sandbagged doors, and cars found themselves axle-deep in water. The city's newest restaurant, after only four days' trading, had to close that Saturday as high seas demanded a heavy toll. The Waterfront Restaurant on the Hoe suffered hundreds of thousands of pounds of damage.

At a time when 999 was the number of the night, a bitter pill of irony had to be swallowed at Sidmouth in East Devon. There a vital rescue service was ordered to stand down. There was no alternative because the 12-strong Sidmouth Inshore Rescue Service was made homeless as 50 foot waves almost demolished their brick-built premises at The Ham. The members' inflatable rescue boat was buried under tons of rubble as were the VHF radio equipment and wetsuits.

It was indeed a long, long trail of damage awinding along the peninsula. At nearby Seaton the town's sea wall, built eight years previously, was tested to the full, but still failed to keep thousands of gallons of sea water from flooding the Esplanade.

For Teignmouth it was a story of the worst flooding for 20 years with breakers smashing over the sea wall, flipping heavy coping stones aside, smashing windows and kiosks, and in Totnes the roof of a house in Bridgetown was ripped off. Who was to know how many would follow?

There was the sea, the sand, the shingle, all mixed into a cocktail of destructive power by the merciless wind. Wooden structures were unceremoniously shattered; part of the sea wall was swept away at Hope Cove; quays were flooded; roads were closed; and the main London to Penzance railway line was breached near Teignmouth.

Everyone swore they had never known a weekend like it, and when the tumult subsided they breathed a sigh of relief while counting the costs.

St Ives MP David Harris toured the Mount's Bay area and called for government money for sea defences. "I don't think anyone can begin to estimate the cost of the damage, but I am sure it will run into millions of pounds," he said. He was right, naturally, but like the rest of us did not have a crystal ball and could not foresee the weeks that lay ahead. Perhaps it was just as well.

That weekend before the presents were unwrapped, the turkeys carved, the carols sung, and the seasonal toasts of goodwill tippled was nowhere near the end of an unequal fight against the elements. Little did the people of a bruised and bloody-nosed region realise it was just the first round.

– Hurricane Force –

Nobody can say we were not warned. Unlike the "hurricane" of 1987, when the English engaged in one of their favourite occupations, recrimination with the advantage of hindsight, the meteorologists told us exactly what we could expect.

The London Weather Centre, on the night of January 24, 1990 explained that a 24 hour spell of severe weather was on its way as a deep low pressure area moved east across the Channel. "Further south over England and Wales a spell of heavy rain will make driving difficult. The problem will be enhanced by gales or severe gales, and structural damage is expected," — that was the message.

Plymouth Weather Centre forecast severe gales developing in the morning and said that in exposed places the winds could reach 100 miles per hour. Nothing could be clearer and the only quibble one might have — again with the advantage of hindsight — is about another English trait, a penchant for the understatement.

As it turned out, Thursday, January 25 was the day when we all had a nightmare in broad daylight. Not even hyperbole was sufficient to describe the screaming, banshee-echoing gales, hurricane force, that this time scarred the South West in such a way that it literally altered the face of some of the landscape for years to come.

Not just destruction on a vast scale, but death too was a tragic ingredient of the day's blistering, blustering, boisterous blow that seemed to wail on and on like a tormented spirit and which plunged so much of the region into darkness for days and days.

At the height of this unbelievable catastrophic bombardment police pleaded with drivers to stay off the roads, admitting their manpower was "stretched to the limit". Small wonder as trees — the biggest killers and the biggest casualties — toppled like nine pins, a million of them uprooted in Devon and Cornwall alone, crushing cars, smashing down power and telephone lines, and tearing the roofs off so many properties that only the insurance companies kept count.

26. **opposite page:** *Lovely old churches like this one at Hatherleigh suffered devastation.*
27. **below:** *This massive old tree at Woodbury Salterton is to become the school's emblem — the youngsters will never forget the storm.*

28. **right:** *Lorries were blown over like Dinky toys — this casualty was at Countesswear near Exeter.*
29. **below:** *Sailors had to mess about with boats at Velator near Braunton in a different way during the storm.*

Walls collapsed, chimneys crumbled, fences either floated away or were flattened, and windows shattered as gust after gust mortar-fired a wave of attacks like a massive army against a very vulnerable and besieged target.

Throughout the country 46 people died that day, and sadly the Westcountry contributed to the tale of sorrow. A seaman drowned off Lands End, a tree fell on a car at Newquay killing the driver, another one came crashing down at South Brent killing a man in its path, and at Torquay it was the same story — another tree down and another victim to mourn.

Those ghastly gusts topped 117 mph and apart from those that died others were severely injured, some were superficially hurt, and many escaped harm by the skin of their teeth. To be out on that day was to be at risk whether from those treacherous trees, dropping like sufferers of a sudden plague, broken branches, falling masonry, slates and tiles slicing through the air with a deadly cutting edge, or from shards of shattered glass. Fear was as fierce as the wind for some and with very good reason. Children from scores of schools had to be got home to safety because of ruined or vanished roofs.

But it could — hard though it was to believe at the time — have been so much worse. In mid-Devon, to take just a couple of incidents, hundreds of youngsters escaped because the roofs of two schools parted company with the walls minutes before classes started. Then a tree crashed on a school bus bound for the Queen Elizabeth Community College in Crediton. A 12-year-old boy had to be rushed to hospital, but it was an asthma attack brought on by shock.

There were so many similar misses. At Bickleigh first school near Tiverton a flat roof was wrenched off and although one class helper did have a broken arm, as the headmaster Roy Kerrigan commented with relief: "Half an hour later and that room would have been filled with about 30 children."

For quite a while getting anywhere was virtually impossible. At one stage almost every main road in Devon was blocked to some extent, and rail passengers between Exeter and Plymouth had to get off either at St David's or Newton Abbot because of the hammering the line was taking as it snaked its way along the coast between Dawlish and Teignmouth. Brymon Airways, whose planes normally fly between Newquay, Plymouth and Gatwick, cancelled all their daytime flights, and Britanny Ferries had to cancel sailings from Plymouth to Roscoff.

30. Not even helicopters, like this toppled chopper at Weston Super Mare, could stay on the ground.

31. ***right:*** *Over a million trees came down — these were at Mount Edgcumbe Park.*

32. ***below:*** *A tree crashes into the roof of this house in Gyllyngvase Terrace, Falmouth.*

33. **left:** *Even a police car was flattened by the gales in Torquay.*
34. **below:** *A tumbling branch meant ambulance treatment for a stall holder at Axminster Market.*

35. **opposite page:** *Wet, windy, but still working well — the electricity men all over the South West.*
36. **left:** *A SWEB engineer tackles the task of getting the power back at Noss Mayo.*
37. **below:** *The Marines get stuck in to remove fallen lines at Exton, near Exeter.*

City centre streets all over the region were closed because of the fusilade of tiles, masonry or scaffolding being ripped away and ricocheting around. When part of the roof of Truro Cathedral went, police made the streets around a no-go area. The most serious damage was to the main roof of the nave and an area of the north transept 100 feet above the ground. The Dean, the Very Rev David Shearing, said: "The wind was so strong it almost shook the building. One could feel the whole place moving. It was quite alarming."

Part of the glass roof at Truro bus station was blown in and David Glendenning was in the garage when the roof caved in. "There was an almighty roar and a crash and we looked up to the skylight. It looked like Jesus in the shape of a 10 feet by 12 feet sheet of glass falling towards us. It hit a mini bus which was parked in the garage," he said.

Inevitably it was a bad day to be driving anything, but especially a high-sided vehicle — the wind overturned so many as if they were nothing more than Dinky toy playthings. Caravans were easy prey as well. They scattered all over the place, but at Perranporth for example nearly 70 were badly damaged as they were torn from their standings, some sent careering through a neighbouring site. An eye-witness said: "It looks like a battlefield with the wreckage strewn around — it is terrible to see."

There were many battlefields. Everywhere it was the same story, be it houses, churches, schools, hospitals, old people's homes, offices, chalets, shops — a catalogue of damage that grew steadily from early morning, throughout the day, and into the night.

Plenty of people were evacuated because of danger and too many were made temporarily homeless because, until repair work could be carried out, their properties were simply not safe. Even soccer discovered a different kind of hooligan. Half of Torquay United's main grandstand roof blew off — a terrible setback considering the stand had only been rebuilt a couple of years before.

You could not even have a cup of coffee in peace, as the staff of one of the Westcountry's top hotels found, nearly to the cost of life and limb. At the Polurrian Hotel, Mullion, which faces the sea on the Lizard peninsula, eight members of staff were getting things ready for the re-opening in April. They were just having a coffee break when the chimney was blown through the roof. One of them was trapped in the falling rubble.

Tale after tale like this came flooding into *The Western Morning News* newsroom where staff burned the midnight oil with a vengeance, piecing together the picture of a climatic clobbering, its like not known within living memory. It was the sort of day when everyone had a story to tell,

38. Many had lucky escapes — such as when this school bus was hit by a tree at Newton St Cyres.

most seeming to start: "Heavens! Was I lucky? . . ." But unhappily there were so many who were not.

Yet mid-afternoon city centre car parks were unusually empty for a Thursday — an indication not of dereliction of duty but of people having to rush home to try and arrange repairs or offer help to relatives and friends.

Perhaps as good a description of the day as any came from Exeter Automobile Association patrolman Chris King: "It is absolutely horrific — a nightmare. People have been opening their car doors and seeing them wrapped around the front of the vehicles. I saw the roofs of three houses just peel off and disintegrate in Cowley Bridge," he said.

A police spokesman in Plymouth put it equally as well but rather more bluntly. Describing the situation in one particular road near the Hoe, he said: "All hell has broken loose." Indeed it had, right across the South West and on further up into the country that venomous tempest extracted its terrible Danegeld of damage and death.

Nobody really knew that night how bad it had been. People were in the dark figuratively as to the details of the wind's will and testament, and in tens of thousands of cases, simply physically in the dark. At the height of the storm the 132,000 volt power line into Devon and Cornwall was cut. Another way of putting it is the national grid failed at Plymouth, and a large slice of the city and the whole of Cornwall were instantly cut off.

So at one stage 400,000 homes in the South West were without electricity, and although the grid was only out for two hours, when it came to the low voltage network along minor roads and back lanes, the South Western Electricity Board had to rely on customers ringing in and reporting faults.

They were, of course, swamped, and 24 hours after the storm there were still 110,000 people without power — 50,000 of them in Cornwall, 35,000 in Devon and 25,000 in Somerset. SWEB had prepared itself for trouble and contingency plans snapped into action. But as they built up a picture of their wrecked supply system it was clear their own 1,000 outdoor staff could not cope alone.

39. Even homes were turned topsy-turvy, and caravans like this one in North Cornwall were easy prey for the wind.

*40. **above:** Chimneys crumbled like this one at Millbridge, Plymouth.*

*41. **below:** Greenhouses, like this one at Saunton, North Devon, collapsed in shattered heaps.*

What followed was misery for the consumers and the most amazing battle by a dedicated army of electricity workers, beavering in appalling conditions, snatching only a few hours sleep when they could, to put the lights back on in the peninsula. It was not, however much one might have wished, just a case of changing a fuse. The power lines lay buried under fallen trees, transformers had caught fire, poles were flattened, and live cables, capable of killing the unwary, lay on the ground. As Devon's area manager George Ashwood put it: "It had blown like hell. The work was hazardous. We could not go charging in like the cavalry."

At the start of the massive operation a small but useful force of 25 Royal Marine commandos from Taunton — all that could be found because the marines were on exercise in Norway — helped clear fallen trees. Other electricity boards in the Midlands and North answered appeals for engineers. Public companies and Eire electricity workers also responded. By air and sea the Irishmen and all their equipment arrived in Devon and Cornwall.

As the days went by the workforce rose to 1,400 and boards in the south of England, their own storm damage repaired, were drafting in more. Outside engineering staff — the men who climb the poles and rig the wires — were working a 15 hour day. At night a team of engineers in the operations room planned work for the following day.

It was tough, energy-sapping, exhausting work for the engineers, but for the people who experienced over a week without power the novelty soon wore off and became instead worrying hardship.

42. Getting anywhere was hard work — especially when the winds demolished signs like these at Marsh Mills.

Nostalgia is all very well in small doses, but those who tend to harp on about the old days of oil lamps, roaring fires and meals cooked on a Cornish range, black as widow's weeds, tend to forget people just do not have such lamps anymore, or quaint Cornish ranges, and that this is the day and age of central heating and all the other things of life which need electricity.

But it had to be make do and mend with candles and gas camping cookers. Desperate householders had no choice but to turn back the clock, but as ever villagers and townspeople rallied around and proved so refreshingly that in any emergency somehow the best in people rises to the top.

At least the village of Chillaton in Devon, for instance, did have the advantage of a mobile take-away food van which visited from Tavistock. Said Mrs Caroline Parker of the village post office: "Everyone who did not have a Rayburn turned out in the middle of the village for their tea. We would have been really stuck without him." She reflected ruefully: "It makes you wonder how on earth they managed years ago with just candles."

Albert and Armimal Fox, who live in nearby Coryton, said their only means of cooking had been by a tiny camping stove and the open fire. "We have been living off sandwiches and soup. It is really bad because not only have we no heating, but we cannot get hot water either," said Mr Fox.

Frances Carpenter, who comes from Horrabridge, said: "We have a small kettle by the open fire to heat the water and we keep the teapot there to keep it warm. You do not realise just what it is like until you are thrown into it like this."

Yes there was a lot of rallying around, all sorts of agencies weighed in with help, there was community spirit and maybe it was cosy in the village pub where the beer could flow because the pumps were pressurised and did not need electricity. But there was worry and discomfort, food from deep freezes to be ditched, and the whole business was thoroughly uncomfortable and utterly miserable for those who had to endure it.

*43. **opposite page:** Some things had to be made safe in a hurry — in Camborne the ornamental turret of the old fire station had to come down.*
*44. **below:** Tumbling masonry was another hazard, and this scene at West Hoe, Plymouth, was typical.*

– The Stormy Deluge –

It was one of the Bard's many monarchs, King Lear, who ranted "Blow, winds, and crack your cheeks; rage, blow, you cataracts and hurricanes, spout till you have drenched our steeples, and drown'd the cocks." During December, January, and February of the winter of '89/90 the advice was certainly heeded by the British weather. Other than a few respites it scarcely seemed to stop blowing, and the rain, as the Cornish say, came down "like stair rods".

Hammering against the window panes, kicking high in the streets, swirling and sweeping in the glare of headlights, it left the South West soaking, saturated, and as soggy as a sponge.

Time and again roads were flooded, pastureland turned into lakes, and rivers, so desperately low in a summer that had brought a drought, ran in ribboned torrents. By February some were flowing at five times the rate they would normally register at that time of year.

Calamity of one kind or another was always around the corner, even if the hazel trees were bedecked in their necklaces of catkins, snowdrops and crocus were flowering along with the camelias, and daffodils were piercing through the ground with their spears, anxious to declare it was spring. Mild enough, of that there can be no doubt, but the wild and wet weather refused to be upstaged, and so many times the weathermen told us there was another strong blow or drenching on the way. It almost became repetitious. The coastal flooding that accompanied the monstrous seas of December had a partner in the deluge inland.

On Wednesday, December 20 the heavens opened with a vengeance and those winds got up again, reaching 75 mph at Falmouth, thankfully well below the speeds of the previous weekend. But as the rain slanted down — more than an inch in Plymouth and Exeter that night and one and a half inches at Princetown — so the rivers rose and flood warnings went out. Cornwall, this time, escaped with less — only three quarters of an inch on Bodmin Moor.

*45. **opposite page:** Making trees safe was a tricky job for this tree surgeon at Torquay.*
*46. **below:** The weather was strictly for the birds as could be seen when the river Exe burst its banks at Stoke Canon.*

But in Devon, mainly the east and south of the county, conditions were such that an army of 300 council workmen with 100 machines tackled the clean-up operation that followed severe road flooding.

While the winds might have seemed small beer to what had gone before, they were strong enough for the lighthouse keeper at Start Point to abandon his home when heavy seas demolished 40 feet of cliffs. The old engine house was destroyed and lighthouse keeper Brian White had to move out of his home because it could have been undermined by the cliff falls.

Newton Abbot was saved from flooding — it suffered cruelly a decade before when more than 700 properties were inundated — by the Holbeam dam flood control on the river Lemon. That Wednesday night more than 22 million gallons of water were diverted into the flood retention dam. By any standards that would seem enough, but in February it was in action again, this time holding 40 million gallons.

Sidmouth and Exmouth were a couple of the places that bore the brunt of the downpour, and a Sidmouth family were forced out of their home over Christmas because of the severe flooding. They were the only householders in East Devon who had to be rescued by firemen although more than 100 properties in the district knew the trauma of flood water.

A stream running alongside the car park of a thatch-roofed Colyton inn became a torrent and because a culvert was not big enough to take the water it flowed over the top of a three foot wall, putting the bar and seven other downstairs rooms under a foot of water.

Then, weeks later, still reeling from the great storm of January 25 — nobody would forget the start of this decade, or the end of the other one come to that — the South West suffered another of nature's nasty little tricks. It was just 24 hours later while those SWEB engineers were fighting to restore supplies in West Cornwall that a freak lightning bolt smashed into a transformer, plunging homes back into darkness. Many were the setbacks they had to experience.

47. A lakeside view of the flooded Exe Valley just outside Exeter.

Incredibly people at Princetown, still coping with candles, could scarcely believe their eyes when they woke to find a blanket of snow — well, at least it brought some smiles to the eyes of children, and cynically it could be said to have made a change.

Three days later the weather turned testy again as once more driving rain turned many of the area's rivers into swollen and roaring torrents and flooding threatened to a familiar accompaniment of howling winds. Another crop of flood warnings went out and in gusts of 90 mph in exposed places, stormy seas washed over sea defences at Teign Grace, Par, St Ives and Penzance. Still the weathermen could offer us "naught for our comfort" and warned (as if we did not know): "We are not out of the woods by any stretch of the imagination." The spectre of more structural damage loomed again for the South West and indeed for the whole of what was dubbed "battered Britain".

It was "be prepared" time and again as more than a dozen Torquay residents were evacuated from their homes when a swaying weathervane blackmailed a possibility of crashing down from a church, and an Exeter school had to close because of the risk of scaffolding falling from a nearby church there.

The menace for the Cornish village of Calstock somehow seemed more sinister. There, twenty-five people were forced from their beds when hundreds of tons of rubble threatened their homes after a landslide. The shocked residents fled in the early hours after two thirds of a garden collapsed down the cliffside.

This 2.00 am drama started when Chief Superintendent Nick Crowhurst, who lives in the village, received a telephone call from a neighbour who said her garden had disappeared. Superintendent Crowhurst promptly evacuated nearby residents to his own home and his wife Sandra put the kettle on. She sat everyone around an open fire while she laid on tea from a camping stove — the blackout was still on.

48. When the Taw and Torridge broke their banks, the North Devon countryside looked more like the Lake District.

49. *right:* There was a lot of mopping up to do — as Ron Shopland, landlord of Plymouth's Three Crowns, discovered.

50. *below:* Nothing like a chat in a flooded Cornish street to pass away the time.

51. *opposite page:* A woman's work is never done, especially after flooding.

52. *Crossing the street at Looe was a problem, even when the lights were red.*

53. *In Looe the flooding made shopping a soggy chore.*

54. A wet and windy rush hour home in Plymouth.

55. It might be fun for these youngsters at Otterton, but it was no pleasure for most when the floods came.

41

Age-old quips about "it never rains but what it pours" had long ceased to be funny, but the deluge went on. On Wednesday, February 7 flood warnings went out for nine South West rivers, and a South Devon primary school was forced to evacuate its 230 pupils when the water came within feet of the classrooms. Parents at Dartington primary school collected their children just after midday. Bidwell brook, which runs through the school's grounds, had burst its banks and the swirling waters posed increasing safety problems.

Wet and weary, people seemed to be asking the same question every day — will it never stop? Memories being notoriously short, few bothered to recall that in the summer we were querying whether it would ever rain.

There were lulls in the storms, brief though they may have been, and the rainfall figures speak their own eloquent testimony of how things were. It was wet enough in December — Exeter, for example, notched six inches of rain which was nearly double what the city would normally get that month, and in fact everywhere the rainfall was well above average.

January was a similar story, with Princetown having 16 inches of rain, virtually double the amount it would normally get that month, and Bastreet, on Bodmin Moor, had 13 inches, which is 75 per cent above average.

Then, in the first 14 days of February, Exeter, with five inches, had already doubled the amount of rain it should receive in the entire month, while Bastreet, drenched by 12.25 inches, had had 150 per cent more than it would usually get in February.

But before Valentine's Day, the South West braced itself for yet another onslaught. True, the forecasts were not as dire as they had been before, but this time the wind was to come from another direction — a cold north to north westerly that above 1,000 feet could bring snow.

On Sunday, February 11 storm force winds gusting up to 80 mph hit the region, bringing more flooding, more structural damage — nowhere near on the same scale — and leaving 3,000 homes

*56. **below:** Sandbags helped some, but were not enough to keep the floods at bay for hundreds of properties.*

*57. **opposite page:** Cars were axle-deep in flood water when flooding hit parts of Plymouth.*

without electricity. In Sidmouth a seafront hotel was left without a roof when a 40 foot section was ripped off, and thousands of pounds of damage was caused as it crashed onto the forecourt.

The worst devastation was at poor Mousehole, which had been on the receiving end of so much of the sea's savagery in December. The previous storm, tempest, and flood paled into insignificance when the village was hit by a whirlwind.

The spiralling mass of air, whipped up by a severe thunderstorm, ripped through roofs, greenhouses and garden sheds. The harbour front was literally in the front line of the freak weather with 20 roofs damaged. Police Constable Doug Trethowan described the whirlwind as "terrifying", while newsagent Dave Redhead said: "There was one almighty whoosh and everything took off. There were bits of rooftop and chimney stacks flying everywhere. I was amazed nobody was killed or badly injured."

The rain that day was so torrential all phone lines at Brixham coastguard station were knocked out, but although the winds whistled past Berry Head at nearly 90 mph, it took just four minutes to get those phones back again. British Telecom had fought its own noble battle this winter.

During the night the weather abated but river levels were still high enough to force British Rail to suspend services between Taunton and Exeter after the river Exe burst its banks. On that Monday morning the damage was being assessed once more. For all that it was nothing like as bad as had been experienced before, still tens of thousands more trees had come down, more slates flew from the roofs, and more fences listed drunkenly.

Chris Morrow of the Forestry Commission's "windblow information desk" summed it up as a case of "rubbing salt into the wounds".

58. **above:** *Over the water, and into more as motorists drove off the Torpoint ferry.*
59. **opposite page, above:** *Keeping the road clear in Cornwall from the sand as well as the sea.*
60. **opposite page, below:** *To everyone's surprise even snow hit Princetown, and the snowploughs had to be called out.*

61. **above:** *The flooding on the river Tamar,*
near Gunnislake bridge.

62. **below:** *Pastures, like these at Otterton,*
East Devon, turned into lakes when the
heavens opened.

63. **above:** One of the loveliest churchyards in the country, St Just In Roseland looked a mess after the storms.

64. **below:** Evacuation was the order of the day at Calstock when a landslip threatened these houses.

On Valentine's Day the South West Region of the National Rivers Authority issued a statement which neatly encapsulated much of what the region had gone through, and why its people were sick and tired of battling against the elements. That organisation was only formed in September and yet since then — the bulk between mid-December and that special day for romantics — its flood warning office had been in operation 600 hours. The flood watchers, pouring over their weather radar screens, had issued over 120 flood warnings. An awful lot of water had flowed under a great many bridges.

As for the cost of it all, that was still being counted as the claim forms dropped like confetti through the post boxes of insurance companies. It was known that local authorities alone in the Westcountry faced repair bills of more than seven million pounds, and one national estimate was that the insurance companies were preparing to pay out in excess of two billion pounds. But, of course, there were so many who were not insured, and so the true financial cost of the winter's damage will never really be known. Indeed those bills continued to mount as frantic February neared its end. Once more the warning was to batten down the hatches as violent storm force 11 winds screamed along the north coast, bringing high tides crashing over sea defences.

While other parts of the country bore the brutal brunt of this onslaught, and the wicked winter death toll grew, again trees came down, roofs were damaged and North Devon suffered some nasty tidal flooding.

Around 50 homes at Appledore, near Bideford, were flooded, and Bideford Quay was under three feet of water. Lynmouth was also hit by flooding as was Ilfracombe where 20 houses and two hotels were awash.

For SWEB it was a by now familiar case of working in atrocious conditions to restore power to more than 2,500 homes, while an equally tough job faced men at the South Hams village of Beesands. The £100,000 task there was to repair breached sea defences and it involved bringing in 6,000 tons of giant boulders, each weighing up to eight tons.

The weather, like *Gone With the Wind* — and how people wished the wind had gone — was proving to be an epic that went on and on.

*65. **opposite page:** British Telecom had their own massive battle to fight to get the phone lines buzzing again.*
*66. **below:** Farm workers lead a flock of sheep to safety from the swirling flood water at Frogmore Farm, near Cullompton.*

*67. **above:** The cost of this car on the outskirts of Torquay is clear — but nobody could put a value on lost trees.*

*68. **below:** Workmen clear an oak after a driver was rescued on the Honiton to Ottery St Mary road.*

– A **L**andscape Changed –

When hundreds of thousands of elm trees fell prey to that pernicious little pest, the Scolytus beetle — another way of saying Dutch elm disease — it was described as an environmental disaster in the South West. After the great storm which claimed at least one million trees in Devon and Cornwall, and four million nationally, nobody used that expression.

But, as Giles Clotworthy of the National Trust at Lanhydrock gazed out across the superb 30 acre garden now a scene of amputated trunks and severed limbs, he talked of a landscape that had changed.

Looking at a picture repeated at other of the Trust's magnificent gardens, he said: "In our garden we have lost about a thousand trees and there are others so damaged they will have to come down."

His judgement was simple and not overstated: "Large parts of the familiar and well loved landscape of the county have been altered. It is unprecedented. We have never experienced damage on a scale like this, and there are some heart-rending scenes."

It was a verdict with which nobody disagreed, least of all John Hunt, district forestry officer of the Forestry Commission for Somerset and South Devon. The Commission — when those winds which had acted like a giant lumberjack gone berserk permitted — flew aerial surveys to get a clear picture of the damage.

Again the word was "unprecedented" and in just one area, from East Dorset to Dartmoor, but not including the moor, about 250,000 trees were down, the equivalent of a year's cut of 60,000 tons of timber with a value of over £2 million.

69. When trees came down they had to be cleared. David Jackson gets to work at Mannamead, Plymouth.

What could not be valued was the harm that had been caused to environmental habitat. Mr Hunt had seen a herd of deer in battered Haldon Forest wandering dazed and disorientated — baffled bambies bewildered by what had happened. And how could anyone place a cost on those mature trees of up to 200 years old that had graced the South West's historic and beautiful gardens and so many of which now like corpses were strewn on the ground, uprooted, branches a twisted tangle of fractured timber?

At the height of the storm of January 25, gardeners in those famous places could only stay indoors and watch dismayed as the gales snuffed out years of work. It was too dangerous by half to venture into arborial areas which were being wrecked before their eyes.

When they could try to find a way through blocked and barricaded paths the sorry story began to take shape. At Antony House among the timbered treasures four 200-year-old Lebanese cedars had been lost and the woodland garden devastated. Part of the valley garden at Cothele had been flattened, and at Trelissick, that lovely garden above the King Harry Ferry, where heliotrope is a tradition, 200 trees had gone.

At Lanhydrock itself holes were punched into the shelter of beeches grown to protect the gardens, and many were lost in the famous avenue of beeches leading to the house.

These casualties were just spotted in a snap-shot assessment before it had been possible to reach the wooded areas of land beyond the gardens themselves.

Said Mr Clotworthy: "In places it looks as if a giant's hand has cut a great swathe through. It will take, not weeks, but years to clear it all up."

In Devon, where the Trust owns 30,000 acres, it was the same story, and Sally Twiss of Killerton declared: "It is a disaster. We have lost thousands of trees." At Killerton, where, just outside Exeter in the 1770s John Veitch, one of the great landscape gardeners, set about the task of creating this splendid one on a hill with woods around, over 80 trees tumbled. One was an Arbutus, which was the largest of its kind in the country, and another was a rare Thuga, one of the first of its kind to be planted in England.

It was not just the trees, body blow though that was, for only time would tell what plants and shrubs had been crushed beneath their mighty weight.

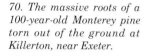

70. The massive roots of a 100-year-old Monterey pine torn out of the ground at Killerton, near Exeter.

At Saltram, near Plymouth, some of the 19th century limes in the avenue leading to the George II mansion, with its magnificent interior plasterwork and decoration, had thundered to the ground. Mount Edgcumbe Park too had been savaged with 800 trees lost at least, while at Coleton Fishacre garden near Kingswear, renowned for its tender plants and shrubs, several of the Monterey pines, which formed a shelter belt to the garden, were blown down. This was something which would alter the micro-climate of the garden irretrievably.

Although the task of clearance was monumental, action was swift, with the first priorities to make safe what was still dangerous — split trunks and swaying branches — and to record what had been lost. There were cuttings to be taken of the rarest victims so they could be grown again for future generations.

Top officials of the Trust journeyed to the South West to see for themselves, and the trees and gardens storm disaster appeal launched after the hurricane of 1987 was opened again.

In that year £2 million was raised by public appeal and Mr Clotworthy thought a sum of about the same order would be needed this time, with a fair proportion of that cash likely to come to the South West.

John Sales, chief gardens officer for the Trust, declared Devon and Cornwall the worst hit areas. While the '87 storm had been more localised, this time the damage to gardens had been more spread out.

"But we have to count our blessings. No one garden was annihilated, but parts are very badly damaged," he said. The costs of putting things right were bound to be high because the problems in the parks and gardens were that it was sensitive ground, and clearance work would have to be done carefully or else the gardens could be damaged.

The work of clearing up got underway at once, and ironically as it proceeded so the lawns became carpeted with crocus, and while the chain-saws buzzed like a swarm of stereophonic bees, there were daffodils, primroses, daphnes, rhododendrons and camelias in full flower, proving the resilience of nature.

71. The tangled web of a fallen 150-year-old beech tree toppled at Killerton House.

72. *above:* National Trust gardener Andrew Mudge was only one of many who had a big problem on his hands.

73. *right:* A big clearance task for workmen to clear the Yealmpton to Brixton road.

74. **left:** Saltram House stables took the brunt of this fallen tree.
75. **below:** Another casualty at historic Saltram House, near Plymouth.

76. **above:** *This leafy lane at Red Lion Hill, Brixton, will never look quite the same again.*
77. **right:** *A view of Mount Edgcumbe through gale-fractured timber.*
78. **opposite page, above:** *Another one down — this time at Tedstone House, near Exmouth.*
79. **opposite page, below:** *Damage to a famous avenue of lime trees leading to Saltram House, near Plymouth.*

80. The sea and the land met for a while and it looked as if the ship was going to sail down the street at Plymouth.

81. **above:** *The damage done by flying tin roofs in West Hoe Road, Plymouth.*
82. **right:** *The landscape at Porthleven harbour was not going to look the same for a long time.*

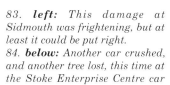

83. *left:* This damage at Sidmouth was frightening, but at least it could be put right.
84. *below:* Another car crushed, and another tree lost, this time at the Stoke Enterprise Centre car park.

85. **above:** *The anger of the sea sweeping against the front at Sidmouth.*

86. **right:** *Repairing the breached sea wall at Lynmouth.*

87. **above:** *Heavy seas pounding Ilfracombe harbour.*
88. **left:** *Sinking feeling! Widespread flooding at Velator, near Braunton.*

Then, however, came another wicked jab to the jaw as those storm force winds of February 11 battered the gardens again, attacking from another direction. Coleton Fishacre suffered once more — a lightning strike split one tree in half — and for gardeners there it was a sudden setback just when they were getting on top.

In Cornwall, Mr Clotworthy sadly reported more trees lost including some fine mature ones which had miraculously survived the first tempest. Of course it was nothing like as bad as had gone before, but as Mr Clotworthy said: "It makes what is left that much more vulnerable. In the long term if this sort of weather is going to be something we look forward to every winter, then Cornwall, lightly treed as it is, is simply not going to see large mature trees." It was a sobering prospect.

For the private gardeners too it was a case of clear up and count the cost, and owners of major parks and gardens were asked to provide storm reports to the Gardens Trust, hopefully the first step in getting government grant aid to help restoration work.

Problems too — like Topsy they just grew this crazy winter — for the wildlife trusts of the two counties.

The Cornwall Trust for Nature Conservation launched its own appeal for funds, reckoning it would cost up to £30,000 to rectify damage on its wildlife reserves. It was inevitable some wildlife would suffer, but the money was needed to clear up and repair paths and boardwalks that had been provided so people could enjoy those reserves.

Trevor Edwards, of the Cornwall Trust for Nature Conservation, explained: "The county has a lot of woodlands derived from coppicing, so it has relatively few old mature trees with standing wood. These are important to nesting birds, invertebrates, and insects. A lot more might have to come down after clearance work so that will become an even more scarce habitat in Cornwall. In the old days you always had plenty of mature trees for the woodpeckers, owls, and bats."

89. Some of the damage at famous Mount Edgcumbe Park.

It was not, happily, all disaster from the flora and fauna point of view. "While storms like this cause damage to some species they bring benefits to others. The damage enables trees and shrubs to come up in the place where the trees have come down," said Mr Edwards.

Both he and Michel Hughes, conservation officer of the Devon Wildlife Trust, urged that where there was no absolute necessity to remove the stricken trees they should be left there. They were, after all, good for invertebrates and fungi.

Mr Hughes voiced another concern regarding the effect of losing so many mature trees. The effect for lichen communities, of which there are some important ones in the South West, could be severe. "Local populations might die out or be severely cut back," he said.

Dartmoor, that last great wilderness, as could well be expected, experienced the full onslaught and fury of the gales, and the price was high. Officials estimated a five per cent loss of its amenity trees — broadleaves in other words — and again not surprisingly the high areas of the moor were the most badly affected. Thousands of trees were down, miles of paths blocked, and historic buildings damaged. Interpretation officer, John Weir, though, struck a note of optimism, a quality shared by all lovers of the countryside and those stoic gardeners. "The impact is severe, but Dartmoor is an amazingly resilient place," he said.

So everywhere the talk was not just about the mammoth task of cutting and clearing away, or gloom about a glut of timber that would knock the prices. It was about replanting and the future, and maybe the chance to improve the environment for the years ahead by the sort of planning and planting that could be done.

For some wildlife, however, it was too late. Those stormy winds had stirred up old deposits of oil — some of it was even vegetable oil lost overboard from ships — and as the sea swirled and swelled so the oil came to the surface, forming tar balls. The result was that thousands of seabirds, mainly guillemots but gannets and others as well, became impregnated with the cloying stuff.

From about Christmas onwards hundreds of birds were washed ashore and then the numbers dropped and they came in in bedraggled dribs and drabs. Hundreds were taken to clearing stations in Somerset and at Perranporth where experience showed Fairy Liquid could not only clean dishes, but was also a mighty good thing for getting rid of the oil on those birds.

RSPCA officials saved hundreds — they had to be released on the north coast because the risk of recontamination on the south was too great — but pointed out that for every bird found alive it was estimated three were dead. That put the death toll at a conservative figure of 2,500.

Sometimes oil was not the culprit — the sheer force of the wind had hurled birds against the cliffs and they were battered to death.

So maybe it was not an environmental disaster as such — man, it seems, with his pollution and development can be a far more ruthless killer of the species which share his planet — but it was a tragedy for the landscape, which can never look as it was before the storms, not in our lifetime at any rate.

90. At least the landscape of the Erme Valley would look the same after the floods went down.

– The Unanswered Question –

The history books are crammed with accounts of great storms of the past, vivid descriptions of the weather causing unheard of events, be it through flooding, gales, thunder, blizzards, or throat-parching droughts. One of the reasons the weather is a favourite topic for saloon-bar small talk in this country is because it always seems so unreliable — as changeable as a lady's whim.

But in this day and age when the environmental debate is, if not at the top, very near it, of every politician's agenda, when global warming is the subject of a host of international conferences, it was inevitable that people would ask whether this winter was a foretaste of what to expect in the future.

Forgetting the more dramatic prophecies of some pundits, there can be no denying there is good reason to postulate at least as to whether those repetitious storms might in some way be connected with the greenhouse effect.

Scientists at the Meteorological Office and the University of East Anglia reported that the Eighties were the earth's warmest years since records began. Alright, the finding provides strong evidence that global warming caused by human activity is already underway as predicted by theory. But the scientists warn it cannot be regarded as conclusive proof.

Now the Ministry of Agriculture, Fisheries and Food cannot be looked upon as a body that goes in for exaggeration. Yet in July last year, when here in the Westcountry we were all being urged to save water, it hosted a conference of engineers, research organisations, universities, and consultants.

Its brief was to examine global warming and its consequences for rivers and coastal zones. A report following that conference underlined the warming that has taken place cannot yet be attributed solely to the greenhouse effect. Other factors like volcanic eruptions, solar variations and ocean current changes also influence climate in the medium and long term.

*91. **opposite page:** It was not the safest thing to do to make a telephone call when this was happening in the storm.*

*92. **below:** A fallen tree at Tedstone House market garden, Lympstone.*

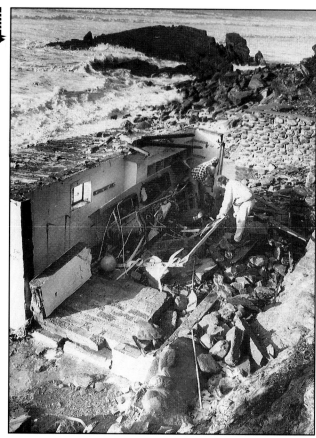

93. *right:* Examining the wreckage at Whitsand Bay Life Club, wrecked by the sea.
94. *below:* Pumping out a boat sunk in the Turf Lock in the Exe estuary.

*95. **left:** A yacht sinking at Turnchapel, Plymouth, as the storms raged.*
*96. **below:** The roaring seas engulf the Waterside Restaurant at Plymouth.*

97. **above:** *Building surveyors check damage to the roof of Queen Elizabeth school, Crediton.*

98. **below:** *Growers suffered badly as greenhouses like this one at Plympton were wrecked.*

*99. **above:** The roof that got away at Plymstock.*

*100. **below:** Coach driver Bill Rimmer had a lucky escape after a tree fell on his vehicle in mid-Devon.*

101. **opposite page:** *A farmer braves the floods at Otterton — but with his tractor he had more chance of getting through.*

102. **left:** *Will scenes like this flooding at Colyford in East Devon become commonplace in years to come?*

103. **below:** *More regular storms like the one which toppled this lorry in North Cornwall are predicted by some.*

On the other hand, said that report, there was general agreement that the rise in global air temperatures will lead to a rise in global sea levels due to the thermal expansion of the oceans and the melting of land-based ice.

This conference was examining the contentious issue because MAFF has good reason to be concerned as it contributes so much money in grant aid to flood defence schemes. Plainly if we are to have higher seas then we are going to need more and better defences.

A summary of the conference said there was general agreement on the ranges for predicted global climate change. The impacts of these changes for rivers and coastal zones would be the rise in sea level, possible increase in storm severity, and changes in weather patterns which could result in greater frequencies of inland flooding and droughts.

Well, here in the South West we have had a drought (those occurred in 1976 and 1984 as well), a handful of severe storms, and a good deal of flooding. And already the newly formed National Rivers Authority was taking into account, when building new coastal flood defence schemes, those global warming predictions that in the next 40 years sea levels will increase by about ten inches.

So, was all this unusual weather linked to the greenhouse effect, carbon dioxide levels, ozone-destroying CFCs, and all the rest of it?

There were many who knew the mercurial nature of the English climate and counselled caution. Well-known North Devon weatherman Bill Tanton summed up the view of a lot of perfectly sensible people when he said: "We have had these extremes before. Looking back over history we have had storms in the 17th and 18th centuries which crossed this country, the like of which had never been heard of before."

104. Rescue services go to the aid of an overturned lorry on Tamar Bridge.

That was most certainly true, and was graphically illustrated by the great blizzard of 1891. It was a storm which not only brought snow so deep that the remnants of the drifts were still there on Midsummer's Day, but death and disaster on an inconceivable scale.

More than 200 lives were lost and more than 60 ships went down between Dover and the Scilly Isles. In Devon and Cornwall, it was said, more than 6,000 sheep and lambs died and half a million trees came crashing down.

The peninsula was cut off, two crack GWR expresses were trapped or derailed, and men with shovels and axes were really the only means of clearing roads or railways. No sophisticated snow-blowers then to keep transport's arteries open.

It had, in fact, been a tough winter that year. Lakes all over the country had ice six inches thick or more. The severe frost killed rabbits and birds, and feathered corpses hung frozen in the trees.

But then February was so dry and springlike, with the primroses out, that the worst, it seemed, had passed. Needless to say, with the British weather, nothing was further from the truth.

It was in March that the blizzard struck with savage suddenness. Men and horses could not stand in the bitter piercing wind, and the drifts built up 20 feet high.

The hurricane and its snow continued for 24 hours, and by then the toll at sea had become a horror story. Even now divers exploring the seabed near Porthallow can still swim over the rusted steel remnants of a ship called *Bay of Panama*. She is the best known victim at sea of the Great Blizzard.

All along the coast the night brought heroism and death — strange how often the two are such close companions. The wind eased on the Wednesday but the snow came back on the Thursday and Friday and more ships were sunk. *Tavy Cleave* was actually filled with 300 feet of snow, and the hills, even in West Cornwall, remained snow-covered in May.

That was a first division storm if there ever was one, and so-called "abnormal" winters there have been aplenty, whether it was 1716 when fairs were held on the frozen river Thames, the post-war ration-rotten misery of the winter of 1947, or the one most of us now remember, the blizzards of 1963.

105. The driver escaped serious injury when his truck was blown off the road at Farway, East Devon.

106. **above:** What a mess when a roof fell on this car in Sutton Road, Plymouth.

107. **right:** Workers at Dunsford Industrial Museum in the Teign Valley clear up after the roof was blown off.

108. **above:** *Caravan parks, like this one in North Cornwall, were victims of the hurricane.*

109. **left:** *Debris everywhere in a battered Plymouth street.*

So it has been with flooding, with this year bringing the 30th anniversary of the great floods of 1960 with its scenes of Army DUKWs washing through the streets of Exeter's St Thomas area that had been turned into turbulent Venetian canals.

Recalling just a few incidents of our weather's armoury of climatic weapons, was this winter merely an assault from one of them? No meteorologist will put his hand on his heart and swear that it is or that it is not. They cannot be blamed, or accused of fence-sitting, because they just do not know.

A Westcountry climatologist for over 30 years described the frequency of this winter's gales as "outstanding". Dr Thomas Revesz, who last year retired as a climatologist at Exeter University's geography department, said: "I think there has been a curious bunching of larger than average gale events." But he stressed it cannot yet be said whether that indicated a long term trend in weather patterns.

110. Plymouth man, Dr Patrick Newell, was assured this tree was safe, but nothing was in this hurricane.

He explained: "Yes there are occurrences of extraordinary events, but you cannot establish a trend over the odd event in a few years. One generation of human beings is nothing. It is like a speck of dust."

In his view there was a possibility that global warming and increased temperature difference was one of the motors of the increased wind activity. It was probably true that the increased

population of the earth and the economic activity were contributing generally to generating more carbon dioxide, but it could not yet be said that we were witnessing climatic change.

Dr Philip Everson, a mathematical meteorologist at Exeter University, said the depressions had come from an area of warm sea in the Atlantic which mixed with the cold air being pulled down from the North Pole. "Something has caused that heat to be there in the Atlantic. It has been there before. It seems to be more intense this time. That could happen by a gap in the ozone layer. That might be what is happening. It could be nothing whatever to do with it. What will happen for future years we don't know. Whether we will have a season like this when we will have a month of very intense winds, we don't know. It is the $64,000 question," he said.

And there it stands. This winter might just go down as producing a great storm that will, from time to time, be recalled in anniversary newspaper articles or television programmes. It might have more significance as the start of something altogether different and not a little frightening.

A climatic hiccup, or the shape of things to come? The answer, as ever, lies in the future, which is always uncertain.

It might, though, be worth the while of mankind, with his pollutant ways, recalling the words of Proverbs 11, v29 which says: "He that troubleth his own house shall inherit the wind."

111. The flooding at coastal resorts — this is Looe — was a misery, but this youngster could manage a smile.

Archive Publications Ltd
10 Seymour Court, Manor Park, Runcorn, Cheshire WA7 1SY
Telephone: 0928-567903

Listed below is the title backlist published by Archive Publications Ltd. They are available from most local book retailers, but if you encounter any problem locating a title, please do not hesitate to contact us at the above address.

Sports Titles

Aberdeen FC	Alastair Guthrie		£6.95
Burnley FC	Tony Durkin		£6.95
Notts County FC	David McVay		£6.95
The Wolves	Martin Swain		£7.95
Blackburn Rovers FC	Peter White		£6.95
Everton FC	Ric George		£7.95
Liverpool FC	Daviod Jones		£7.95
Nottingham Forest FC	Duncan Hamilton		£6.95
Swansea City FC	John Burgum		£6.95
Grimsby Town FC	Geoff Ford		£8.95
Scunthorpe United FC	Bob Steels		£8.95
Wigan RLFC	Leslie Woodhead		£8.95
Widnes RLFC	Leslie Woodhead		£8.95
Nottingham CCC	Nick Lucy		£6.95
Who's Who in British Athletics	Peter Matthews		£8.95
The Golden 80s - a decade of the Cheltenham Gold Cup	John Drinkwater		£9.95

At War Titles

Grimsby at War	Clive Hardy		£6.95
Nottingham at War	Nigel Arthur/Clive Hardy		£7.95
Scotland at War	Ian Nimmo		£7.95
Teesside at War	Malcolm Race		£7.95
Plymouth at War	Keith Scrivener		£6.95
Sheffield at War	Clive Hardy		£5.95
Memories of Swansea at War			£3.95
Tyneside at War	Clive Hardy/Paul Harris		£5.95

Since 1900 Titles

Aberdeen Since 1900	Paul Harris		£6.95
Burnley Since 1900	Keith Fort		£6.95
Swansea Since 1900	Nigel Arthur		£6.95
Blackburn Since 1900	David Allin		£6.95
Edinburgh Since 1900	Paul Harris		£6.95
Sheffield Since 1900	Peter Harvey		£7.95
Glasgow Since 1900	Paul Harris		£7.95
Tyneside Since 1900	Clive Hardy		£6.95

Bygone & Historical Titles

Bygone Merseyside	Derek Whale		£4.95
Edinburgh: The Fab 50's	Paul Harris		£7.95
Leicester in the Fifties			£7.95
Manchester Jewry	Bill Williams		£6.95
Nottingham Then	Ralph Gee		£6.95
Bygone Gloucester	Bill Brunt		£7.95
Edinburgh Then	Hamish Coghill		£7.95
Israel at Forty	Paul Harris		£6.95
Manchester Fire Brigade	Robert Bonner		£7.95
Rotherham Memory Lane	John Tunney		£4.95
THE POLICE! 150 Years of Policing in the Manchester Area	Duncan Broady/Carol Sawkil		£8.95
Grand Old Ladies	Steve Richards		£7.95

General Titles

By Appointment	Paul Harris	£12.95 h/b	£6.95
Disaster!	Paul Harris	£12.95 h/b	£7.95
Bumbles of Mumbles	Alexandra Frith		£4.95